NIKON Z8

USER GUIDE

Unlocking the Potential of the Nikon Z8

A BASIC GUIDE TO OPERATING THE NIKON Z8 CAMERA

FOR BOTH BEGINNERS AND PROFESSIONALS

Joy Joseph

1

Disclaimer and Terms of Use

With every effort, the publisher and author of this book along with the resources included have prepared this work. The correctness, application, fitness, and completeness of the information in this book are not warranted or represented by the author or publisher. This book's content is provided solely for informational reasons. You thereby accept complete responsibility for your conduct if you choose to put the concepts in this book into practice.

Printed in the United States of America

Table of Contents

5

INTRODUCTION

Welcome to the Nikon Z8 compact camera user guide. This tutorial will help you get the most out of your Z8, a powerful and flexible camera that blends cutting-edge technology with easy-to-use settings.

The Nikon Z8 is the peak of Nikon's mirrorless camera technology, with high-resolution imaging capabilities and innovative functionality to fulfill the needs of both professional photographers and enthusiasts. The Z8's superb image quality, rugged construction, and wide feature set enable photographers to take breathtaking photographs and movies in any shooting circumstance.

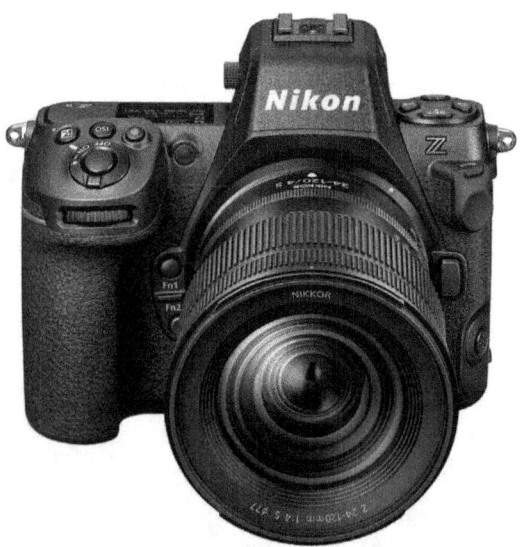

This instruction manual is meant to be a thorough reference for learning and maximizing the Nikon Z8's capabilities. Whether you're a beginner or an experienced photographer, this guide will teach you the skills and techniques you'll need to unleash the Z8's creative potential.

This guide is divided into parts that cover all elements of the Z8, from fundamental setup and functioning to more advanced shooting skills and maintenance. Each section provides extensive instructions, hints, and practical guidance to help you confidently utilize the Z8's features and functionalities.

Before you dive into the Z8's features and functions, be sure you have all of the required accessories and equipment. Charge the battery, attach a memory card, and become familiar with the camera's features and buttons. Keep the user guide ready as you explore the Z8's possibilities.

CHAPTER 1: Getting Started

We'll guide you through the necessary procedures to set up and use your Nikon Z8 camera in this part. These instructions, which cover everything from unpacking to getting to know the camera's functions, will make sure your introduction to Nikon photography goes well.

⊹ Unboxing and contents

> #### Find out what is packaged with the Nikon Z8.

Upon opening the package that contains your Nikon Z8, you will discover a variety of add-ons and necessities:

- Camera body for Nikon Z8
- Strap
- Rechargeable lithium-ion battery EN-EL15c
- battery charger MH-25a
- USB cable UC-E24
- BF-N1 Body Cap
- DK-29 Rubber Eyecup
- Warranty card
- HDMI/USB cable clip

> #### Checked for missing or Damaged items:

Before proceeding, verify each item to ensure it is not missing or damaged. If you notice any anomalies, please contact your merchant or Nikon customer service for help.

↓ Camera Overview

➢ Get to Know the Physical Characteristics:

Examine the outside of the Nikon Z8 camera body for a bit.

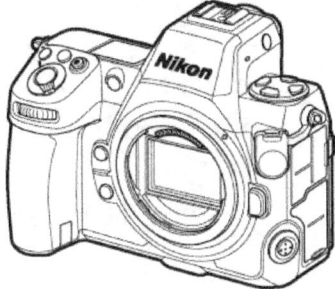

- In front are the autofocus assist lamp, lens mount, and lens release button.
- On top: Control dials, power switch, shutter release button, and mode dial.
- Joystick, control buttons, LCD monitor, and viewfinder on the back.
- Auxiliary terminal cover, memory card slot, and connections are on the sides.

➢ Recognize the Goals and Operations of Controls:

Every port, dial, and button on the camera has a distinct function:

- Buttons: These are used to navigate the camera interface, access menus, and modify settings.
- Dials: Adjust exposure parameters such shutter speed, exposure compensation, and aperture.
- Ports: Use these to connect external devices, such HDMI monitors, microphones, and remote triggers.

✛ Installing and Charging Batteries

➢ Recharge the camera's battery:
To get the EN-EL15c battery charged:

- Put the battery into the charger for the MH-25a.
- Using the included power cord, insert the charger into a power outlet.
- A complete charge will be shown by the battery indicator light turning green.

➢ Install the battery.
To place the charged battery in the camera:

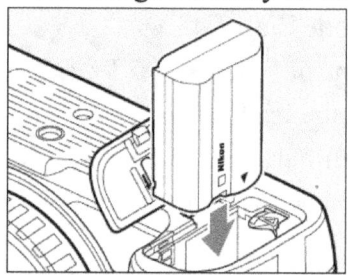

- Unlock the battery chamber door located at the bottom of the camera.
- Put the battery into the container, making that the connections are proper.
- Shut the battery chamber door tightly.

✛ Inserting a Memory Card

➢ Put in an Adequate Memory Card:

Memory cards XQD/CFexpress Type B are compatible with the Nikon Z8.

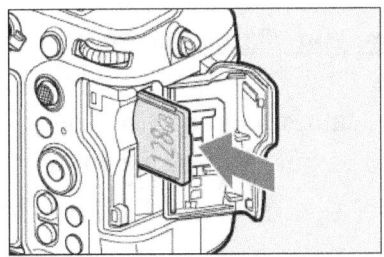

- Find the cover for the memory card slot on the camera's side.
- To access the memory card slot, just slide the cover open.
- Making sure the memory card is properly aligned, insert it into the slot.
- Securely close the lid over the memory card slot.

CHAPTER 2: Camera Setup

⤵ Language and Date/Time Settings

Setting the language, date, time, and timezone will be requested when you turn on the camera for the first time. This is how you do it:

- Turn on the camera by pressing the power switch, which is typically found next to the shutter button.
- Go to the Setup Menu: Press the MENU button on the rear of the camera to bring up the menu system.
- Choose Language: Using the multi-selector (directional pad), go to the "Setup" or "Settings" menu. Find the "Language" or a similar option in this menu. Select it, and then select your favorite language from the list.

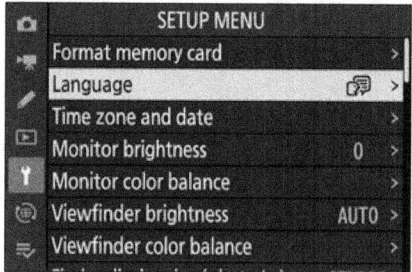

- Establish Date and Time: Use the same menu to get the date and time settings. As necessary, change the date, time, and timezone settings using the multi-selector. Observe the format (month/day/year, for example) and choose the options that correspond to your geographical area.

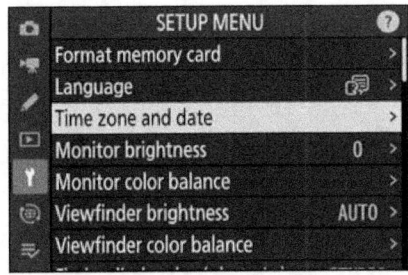

- Confirm Settings: Select the "OK" or "Set" option and click the OK button to confirm your selections after entering the preferred language, date, time, and timezone.

✦ Firmware Updates

Keeping the firmware on your camera up to date is crucial for ensuring optimum performance and software and accessory compatibility. To search for and install firmware upgrades, follow these steps:

- Connect to Computer: Attach your Nikon Z8 to a computer that has internet connection by using the included USB cable.
- Download the most recent firmware: Go to the Z8 downloads page by visiting the support part of the Nikon website. Check if your camera model has any firmware upgrades available, then download the most recent one to your computer.
- Firmware to Camera: After downloading, move the firmware update file to a formatted memory card's root directory.
- Install the most recent firmware: Turn on the camera after inserting the memory card. Go to the camera's setup menu and select the Firmware Update option. To finish the procedure, choose the firmware upgrade

option and adhere to the on-screen directions. During the update, don't take the memory card out or turn off the camera.

✦ Adjust Camera Settings:

Tailor the camera settings to your preferred shooting conditions and style. Here's how to alter the Nikon Z8's settings:

- Open the Setup Menu: To view the menu system on the camera, press the MENU button.
- Go to Custom Settings by navigating: Look for an option called "Custom Settings," "Customization," or anything similar under the settings menu. To access a variety of adjustable options, select this option.

- Investigate Customization Options: You may adjust the camera's focusing, exposure, display, and button assignments by going through the custom settings menu. Investigate these choices at your leisure and modify them to suit your tastes.

- Save Custom Settings: Be sure to save the camera settings once you've adjusted them to your preference. Before you close the menu, look for a way to save or apply the settings changes.

- Reset to Default: The setup menu often includes a feature that allows you to reset all settings of the camera in case you ever need to go back to those initial settings. If you wish to start over after making significant modifications, this might be useful.

↓ Formatting Memory Card:

To make sure a memory card is reliable and compatible with your Nikon Z8, you must format it before using it. This is how a memory card is formatted:

- Memory Card Insertion: Slide the memory card into the slot that is assigned for it by opening the cover. Make sure the card is placed firmly and accurately.
- Click Format Option: To enter the menu system when the camera is powered on, press the MENU button. Look for an option labeled "Format Memory Card," "Format," or anything similar in the settings menu.
- Verify Formatting: After choosing the format option, be sure you really want to format the memory card. Keep in mind that formatting will remove all data from the card, so before continuing, make sure you have a backup of any crucial information.
- Wait for Completion: The camera will wipe the contents on the memory card and have it ready for usage as soon as you approve the formatting. Prior to taking the card out of the camera, let the procedure finish.

↓ Setting up Wireless Connectivity:

With the Nikon Z8's integrated Wi-Fi and Bluetooth capabilities, you can use a smartphone or tablet to remotely operate the camera and share photographs wirelessly. Here's how to configure wifi access:

- To access the Wireless Menu, go to the settings menu and search for the "Wireless" or "Connectivity" option. In order to view the wifi settings, select this option.

17

- Turn on Bluetooth or Wi-Fi: You may choose to turn on Bluetooth, Wi-Fi, or both from the wireless menu. To enable wireless connectivity, select the preferred choice and adhere to the on-screen directions.
- Connect to Smartphone or Tablet: Use your smartphone or tablet to look for accessible networks after turning on Wi-Fi or Bluetooth. To connect, choose the network name (SSID) that matches your Nikon Z8 and adhere to the instructions.
- Install the SnapBridge app for Nikon: Use the Nikon SnapBridge app on your tablet or smartphone to download and install photos and operate the camera remotely. To link your mobile with the camera and utilize its functions, follow the directions on the app.

✦ Lens Mount Compatibility

With its Z-mount, the Nikon Z8 is compatible with a variety of Nikkor Z lenses made especially for Nikon mirrorless cameras. Additionally, F-mount lenses may be used with the Z8 with the use of an extra adaptor. To guarantee compatibility, follow these steps:

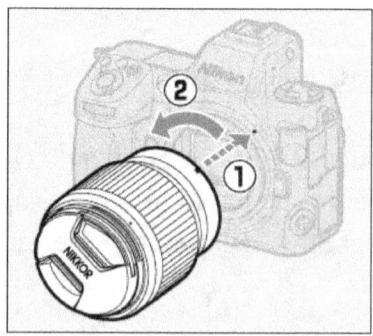

- Using Nikkor Z Lenses: Line up the white dot on the lens and the white dot on the lens mount of your Nikon Z8 to mount a Nikkor Z lens. Till the lens snaps into position, turn it clockwise.

- Using F-mount Lenses with Adapter: The Nikon FTZ Mount Adapter (separately available) is required if you want to utilize F-mount lenses with the Z8. Prior to attaching the F-mount lens to the adapter, attach the FTZ adapter to the Z8's lens mount.

♣ Firmware version check:

To make sure your Nikon Z8 camera is using the most recent software version—which can contain bug fixes, performance enhancements, and new features—you must routinely check for firmware upgrades. To verify the firmware version, follow these steps:

- To access the Firmware Version, go to the Setup menu and choose the "Firmware Version" or a similar option.
- Verify the Most Recent Version: The firmware version that is currently installed on the camera's internal memory will be shown by the device. To find out if an update is required, compare this version number to the most recent version that is listed on the Nikon website.
- Update Firmware if Needed: Download and install the latest firmware version by following the previously given procedures, if one is available.

Chapter 3: Customizing Camera buttons and control

With so many customization choices available for its buttons and controls, the Nikon Z8 lets you adjust how the camera works to your liking. Here's how to alter the controls and buttons:

- Navigate to the Setup menu and seek for an item named "Button/Dial Settings," "Custom Controls," or something similar to access the customization menu.
- Assign Functions: A list of the camera's buttons, dials, and controls may be found in the customization menu. After selecting the button or control you wish to modify, you can give a function to it by selecting one from the list of alternatives.
- Save Custom Settings: After you have given buttons and controls specific functions, make sure you save your custom settings. Before you close the menu, look for an option to save or apply the changes.

⬩ Setting Focus and Exposure Options:

The Nikon Z8 has a range of focus and exposure settings to accommodate diverse shooting situations. Setting focus and exposure choices is done as follows:

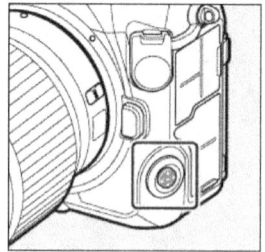

Select the autofocus (AF) mode that best suits your subject and shooting circumstances, including single-point, dynamic, and wide-area AF. Use the menu or dedicated buttons on the camera to access the focus mode options.

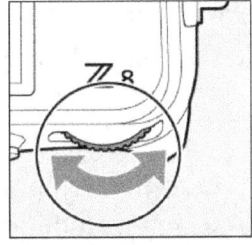 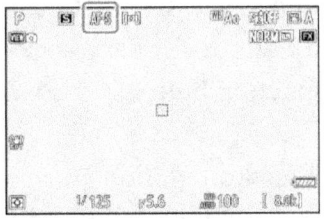

Exposure Mode: Using the mode dial on the top of the camera, choose the preferred exposure mode (manual, shutter priority, aperture priority, etc.). Try a variety of exposure settings to get the desired artistic results.

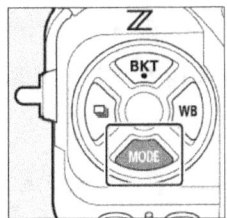

✦ Adjusting Viewfinder and Monitor Settings:

For taking and reviewing photos, the Nikon Z8 has a tilting LCD panel in addition to an electronic viewfinder (EVF). Here's how to change the display and viewfinder settings:

- Viewfinder Adjustment: To guarantee a crisp and clear image, if required, change the electronic viewfinder's diopter setting. To adjust the diopter, turn the dial next to the viewfinder.
- Monitor Brightness: To fit your tastes and shooting circumstances, adjust the LCD monitor's brightness and color balance. Via the menu on the camera, access the monitor settings.

↓ Assigning Function Buttons:

The Nikon Z8 lets you attach certain functions to customizable function buttons for easy access while shooting. Here's how you assign function buttons:

- Function Button Assignment: Go to the Setup menu and select "Function Buttons" or "Assign Fn Buttons."
- Select Function: From the list of possible functions, select the one you wish to assign to a certain button. Commonly assigned duties include ISO adjustment, exposure correction, and focus mode selection.
- Save Settings: Once you've assigned functions to function buttons, save your settings to implement the changes.

↓ Customizing Camera Buttons and Controls

➢ **Button/Dial Customization:**
  Based on your shooting preferences, you may adjust several elements of the camera's functionality, including:
  - Assigning unique functions to certain buttons or knobs.
  - Adjusting the behavior of the command dials for aperture, shutter speed, and exposure compensation.
  - Configuring the multi-selector (directional pad) for menu navigation and focal point selection.

➢ **User Presets (U1, U2, U3):**

The Nikon Z8's mode dial has user preset modes (U1, U2, U3), which allow you to save and quickly recall customized shooting settings. To create user presets:

- Adjust the camera settings (exposure mode, focus mode, white balance, and so on) to your preference.
- Once the settings are specified, go to the setup menu and select "Save User Settings" or "Save/Load Settings."
- Follow the on-screen instructions to save the current settings as one of the user preset modes (U1, U2, or U3).

➤ **Fine Tuning Autofocus Settings:**

The Nikon Z8 has powerful autofocus features, which enable you to fine-tune focusing settings for various shooting conditions. Here's how to improve autofocus performance.

➤ **Autofocus Mode Selection:**
Select the optimal autofocus mode based on your topic and shooting conditions.
- Single-point AF: Use a single focus point to precisely focus on a certain topic.
- Dynamic-area AF: Track moving subjects using multiple focus points.
- Wide-area AF: Use a broader region for general focusing.

➤ **AF-Customization Menu:**
Use the AF-Customization menu to change autofocus settings like:
➤ Focus Tracking Sensitivity: Determine how rapidly the autofocus system responds to changes in the subject's movement.
➤ AF Activation: Choose whether to activate the autofocus system with a half-press of the shutter button or a separate AF-ON button.

✦ Setting White Balance:

White balance adjustment enables correct color reproduction in a variety of lighting settings. Here is how to set the white balance on the Nikon Z8:

- White Balance Presets: Select from a variety of white balance presets, including daylight, cloudy, incandescent, fluorescent, and flash.
- Custom White Balance: Set a custom white balance using a neutral gray or white reference target to ensure accurate color reproduction under specified lighting circumstances.
- Kelvin Temperature: To precisely regulate white balance, manually alter the color temperature using Kelvin values.

✦ Configuring Image Quality and File Format:

Choosing the right picture quality and file format ensures that your images are optimized for various uses. Here's how to set the image quality settings:

- Image Quality: To fit your workflow and editing preferences, you can select RAW, JPEG, or a combination of the two.
- JPEG Compression: Set the degree of JPEG compression to balance image quality and file size.
- RAW Bit Depth: Choose a RAW bit depth (12-bit or 14-bit) for RAW files to capture a broader range of tonal information.

Chapter 4: Shooting mode

⊹ In Auto Mode:

For novices or when you want the camera to automatically adjust all exposure settings, auto mode is ideal. Here's how to make good use of it:

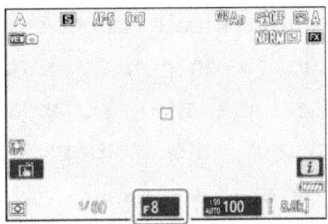

- Place the mode dial on the top of the camera and turn it to the "Auto" (or "Auto" with a green camera symbol) position to set the mode dial to that setting.
- Point and Shoot: To enable the camera to evaluate the scene and make the necessary exposure adjustments after switching to Auto mode, merely frame your photo and push the shutter halfway.
- After taking your picture, examine it on the LCD display and make any required changes to the framing or composition.

⊹ Program Mode

Program option: This option allows you to change other parameters while still having automatic exposure. How to maximize it is as follows:

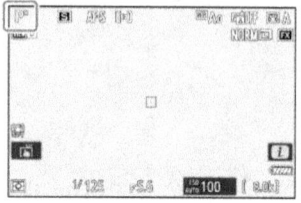

Turn the mode dial to the "P" position to set it to that mode.

- Modify Settings: The camera automatically chooses the shutter speed and aperture while it is in program mode. Nevertheless, you can still use the control knobs and buttons on the camera to change other settings like exposure compensation, white balance, and ISO.
- Experiment Program mode/Play around: Program mode lets you play around with various parameters while still ensuring the right amount of exposure. To control the amount of noise in low-light situations, experiment with different ISO settings or use exposure compensation to change the brightness of your photographs.

⊥ Aperture Priority Mode:

You may manually set the aperture in aperture priority mode, and the camera will adjust the shutter speed to get the right exposure. Here's how to make good use of it:

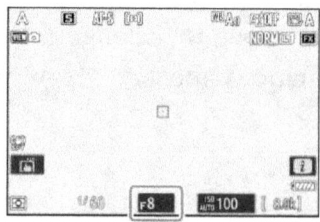

Put "A" or "Av" on the mode dial: Set the mode dial to position "A" (or "Av" depending on the aperture value).

- Choose an aperture: The aperture value may be changed using the main command dial. A bigger aperture (f/2.8, for example) will enable more light to enter the camera and provide a deeper depth of field than a lower f-stop number.
- Modify ISO and Exposure Compensation: To fine-tune the exposure, you may need to modify the ISO sensitivity or utilize exposure compensation, depending on the lighting and desired effect.

⊹ Shutter Priority Mode

When the camera is in shutter priority mode, the shutter speed may be manually adjusted while the aperture is adjusted for optimal exposure. Here's how to make good use of it:

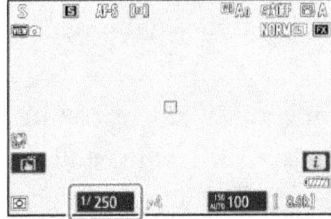

Put "S" or "Tv" on the mode dial: To adjust for time value, turn the mode dial to the "S" (or "Tv").

- Choose the Shutter Speed. The shutter speed may be changed by turning the main command dial. Whereas a shutter speed that is slower permits motion blur, a quicker shutter speed stops motion.

- Consider ISO and Exposure Compensation: You might need to fine-tune the exposure by using exposure compensation or adjusting the ISO sensitivity based on the lighting and intended impact.

✦ <u>Manual Mode (M Manual)</u>

Complete manual control over shutter speed and aperture is available in manual mode. Here's how to make good use of it:

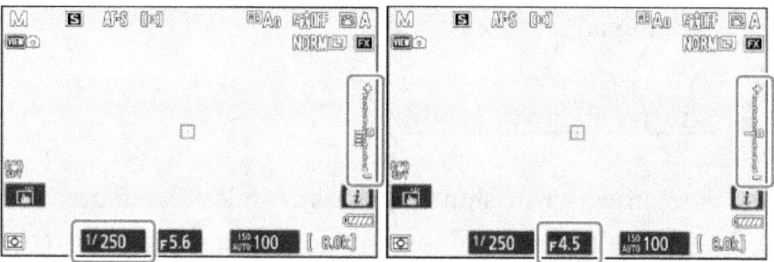

Turn the mode dial to the "M" position to set it to that mode.

- Adjust Aperture and Shutter Speed: When operating in Manual mode, you have to use the main and sub-command dials to manually adjust the aperture and shutter speed, respectively.
- Utilize the Light Meter: Pay attention to the light meter on the LCD panel or in the viewfinder of the camera while you make settings adjustments. For an image that is correctly illuminated, aim to center the meter.
- Try and Practice: Although it takes experience to become proficient, manual mode allows total creative control. To get the desired effect, try various combinations of shutter speed and aperture.

⚜ Custom Modes (C1, C2, C3):

The Nikon Z8 has custom modes (C1, C2, C3) on the mode dial, which allow you to save and instantly recall unique shooting settings. Here's how you utilize custom modes:

- Save Custom Settings: Customize camera settings (e.g., exposure mode, aperture, shutter speed, ISO) for a specific shooting scenario.
- Assign Settings to Custom Mode: Once configured, go to the setup menu and select "Save User Settings" or "Save/Load Settings."
- Select Custom Mode: Rotate the mode dial to the selected custom mode (C1, C2, or C3) to apply the saved changes immediately.

⚜ Bracketing Modes:

Bracketing options allow you to take many photographs at different exposure levels and then merge or choose the best image. Here are the bracketing modes available for the Nikon Z8:

- Exposure Bracketing: Take a sequence of photographs at various exposure settings, usually with shutter speed or aperture changes. This option is ideal in high-contrast scenarios when you want to guarantee that highlights and shadows are properly exposed.
- White Balance Bracketing: Take many photographs with varied white balance settings to ensure correct color reproduction under difficult lighting circumstances. This setting is useful for photographing in mixed lighting conditions.

- Focus Bracketing: Capture a sequence of shots at various focus distances to produce a greater depth of field in post-processing. This mode is great for macro photography or landscape images that require utmost clarity throughout the scene.

Chapter 5: Advance Shooting Features

⊹ High-resolution Sensor:

The Nikon Z8 features a high-resolution sensor that can capture complex details and provide superb image quality. The Z8's high megapixel count makes it ideal for capturing fine details in landscapes, portraits, and other genres of photography that need high picture quality.

⊹ Advance Auto-Focus System:

The Z8 has a sophisticated autofocus mechanism that provides a large coverage area and improved tracking capabilities. Here are a few highlights of the autofocus system:

- The Hybrid Autofocus System combines phase-detection and contrast-detection autofocus to provide fast and accurate focus performance in a variety of shooting scenarios.
- Subject Tracking: Uses complex algorithms to follow and concentrate on moving subjects, resulting in crisp and clear photos even in difficult conditions.
- Eye-Detection Autofocus: Automatically detects and focuses on the subject's eye, resulting in accurate focus and excellent portrait results.

⊹ In-Body Image Stabilization (IBIS):

The Nikon Z8 includes in-body image stabilization (IBIS), which compensates for camera shake and produces clear shots even in low-light circumstances or when using telephoto lenses. Key characteristics of IBIS include:

31

- Five-Axis Stabilization: Corrects camera shake on five axis (pitch, yaw, roll, and horizontal and vertical shifts), offering stability for handheld shooting at slower shutter rates.
- Compensation Range: Provides a large level of stabilization, allowing you to photograph at slower shutter speeds without worrying about blur from camera shake.
- Compatible with All Lenses: Works with any lens attached to the camera, even non-stabilized lenses, to provide consistent stabilization performance throughout your entire lens array.

✦ Advance Metering System:

The Z8 has a sophisticated metering mechanism to properly monitor light and compute the best exposure settings. The key features of the metering system are:

- Matrix Metering: Evaluates the entire scene to find the best exposure depending on variables such as subject brightness, contrast, and color.
- Center-Weighted Metering: Sets priorities for the central part of the frame for exposure estimation, making it suitable for portraits and settings with a strong subject.
- Spot Metering: Measures light from a tiny region in the center of the frame, allowing for accurate exposure adjustment while photographing subjects under difficult lighting situations.

↓ Advance Video Capability

The Nikon Z8 provides sophisticated video recording capabilities for professional videographers. Here are some specifics regarding its video features:

- Bit Depth and Color Sampling: The camera supports high bit depth (10-bit or higher) and color sampling (4:2:2 or higher), resulting in increased color depth and fidelity in video output.
- Log and Hybrid Log Gamma (HLG) Modes: The camera supports logarithmic gamma curves (including N-Log and HLG) for more dynamic range and post-production flexibility.
- Video Assist capabilities: Built-in video assist capabilities like as focus peaking, zebra striping, and waveform displays aid videographers in achieving accurate focus and exposure control.

Chapter 6: Video Recording
⌖ Video Image Area Option:

In the video recording menu, pick [Image area] > [Choose image area] to set the image area for your recordings. The crop utilized for capturing video differs depending on the option picked. Regardless of the setting, the aspect ratio is 16:9.

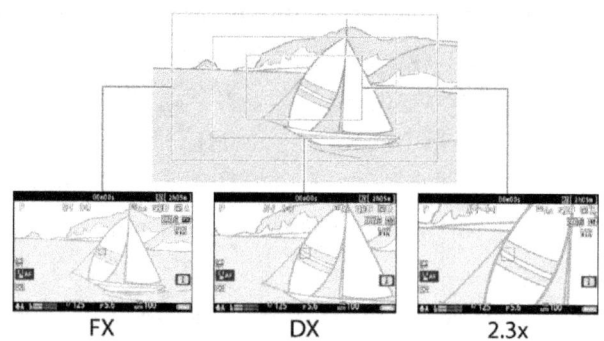

FX   DX   2.3x

- Select [FX] for recording videos in "FX-based video format", and [DX] to film in "DX-based video format".
- The picture area for movies filmed using [N-RAW 12-bit (NEV)] or [ProRes RAW HQ 12-bit (MOV)] chosen as [Video file type] in the film capturing menu is governed by the [Frame size/frame rate] option. The option for [Image area] > [Choose image area] in the film capturing menu is not applicable.
- When using [DX] for [Choose image area] or putting a DX lens on the camera with [3840×2160; 120p], [3840×2160; 100p], [1920×1080; 120p], or [1920×1080; 100p] chosen for [Frame size/frame rate], the apparent focal length increases by about 2.3× when compared to FX format.

  - An symbol on the display indicates which option is presently selected. Selecting [ON] for [Image area] >

[DX crop alert] in the footage recording menu will result in an image-area symbol flashing in the video recording display whenever the DX or 2.3× crop is selected.

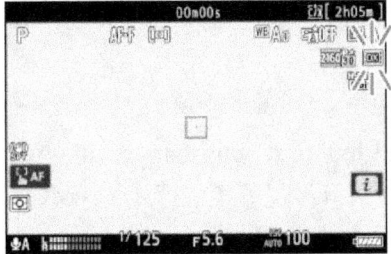

- Choosing [ON] for [Electronic VR] in the film capturing option limits the crop size.

⊥ Points to note when Filming Video

When capturing videos, keep in mind the following points:

- Each movie may be up to 125 minutes long.
- Each video recorded on a memory card containing a storage space of 32 GB or less will be saved as a maximum of eight files. Each of these files will have a maximum size of 4 GB. The number of files and their lengths varies depending on the parameters for [Frame size/frame rate].
- If [ProRes 422 HQ 10-bit (MOV)] is chosen for [Video file format] in the movie shooting menu and the storage device has a storage space of 32 GB or less, recording will stop automatically when the file exceeds 4 GB in size. Videos are not stored in numerous files.
- Depending on the storage card record speed, shooting may terminate before the maximum length is achieved.
- When selecting [N-RAW 12-bit (NEV)] or [ProRes RAW HQ 12-bit (MOV)] for [Video file type] in the video recording menu, video cannot be recorded to SD or XQD memory cards with a capacity of 32 GB or less.

- [Spot metering] is not accessible when video recording.
- The flash illumination (Using a Camera Flash) can't be used.

+ RAW Video

"RAW video" refers to video that was captured with [N-RAW 12-bit (NEV)] or [ProRes RAW HQ 12-bit (MOV)] as the [Video file type] in the video recording menu.

+ Capturing RAW Video

The following limitations is applicable when [N-RAW 12-bit (NEV)] or [ProRes RAW HQ 12-bit (MOV)] is used.

- ISO sensitivities from Hi 0.3 to Hi 2.0 are not accessible.
- The video recording menu does not include [Active D-Lighting], [High ISO NR], [Diffraction correction], [Skin softening], or [Electronic VR] options.
- RAW videos are unable to modified on-camera.
- Regardless of the [HDMI] > [Output resolution] selection in the configuration menu, the highest possible output quality is 1920 × 1080.
- See "Recording N-Log Video" for warnings when using [N-Log] tone mode.

+ Viewing and Editing RAW Videos

RAW movies can only be watched and altered using software for computers that is compatible with the RAW format. Nikon's NX Studio software can only view MP4 proxy videos that were captured alongside RAW footage.

ⵊ HLG Video Recording

Video produced in the Hybrid Log Gamma (HLG) format is suitable for HDR broadcasting and other applications. To record HLG video, in the video recording menu, pick [H.265 10-bit (MOV)] for [Video file format] and then [HLG] tone mode.

- HLG will appear on the shooting display.
- When viewing HLG film, utilize HLG-compatible displays, computers, operating systems, programs, and other equipment to ensure optimal color reproduction.

ⵊ HLG Video Recording Precautions

Photographs shot using [HLG] for tone mode may have more "noise" in the form of randomly spaced bright pixels, fog, or lines than photographs produced with [SDR] or [N-Log].

- The lowest number allowed for the [ISO sensitivity settings] > [Maximum sensitivity] option in the video recording menu is ISO 800.
- The video recording menu's [ISO sensitivity settings] > [ISO sensitivity (mode M)] item has the lowest allowed value of ISO 400.
- ISO sensitivities from Hi 0.3 to Hi 2.0 are not accessible.
- The [Set Picture Control] option in the video capturing menu does not allow you to change Picture Control settings. The [HLG quality] option in the video recording menu allows you to adjust the look of HLG videos.
- The [Active D-Lighting] option in the video recording menu is now set to [Off] and cannot be modified.
- The monitor's display may flicker or be blurry.
- The camera may have difficulty focusing with autofocus, although this does not imply a fault.

＋ HDR (HLR) Output

Optimal color rendition in HDR (HLG) film broadcast over HDMI is only possible if the storage device, monitor, and other devices support HDR. If a signal from the connected device indicates that it allows HDR (HLG), the camera will respond with the identification "gamma: HLG".

➢ Shooting and Camera Playback Display

When [HLG] is used as the tone setting, the image capture and playback outputs in the camera screen and viewfinder may have "noise" in the form of irregularly spaced brilliant pixels, fog, or lines, or they may fail to precisely represent highlights and highly saturated colors. Use HLG-compatible displays, computers, operating systems, programs, and other devices to ensure proper tone reproduction.

➢ HLG Videos Viewing and Editing

HLG movies can only be watched and altered using software for computers that is compatible with the HLG format. Nikon's NX Studio software displays HLG films as thumbnails but cannot be used to watch or modify them.

＋ Hi-Res Zoom

Selecting [ON] for [Hi-Res Zoom] in the film recording menu allows you to zoom in on your subject without losing resolution, even without a zoom lens.

- Hi-Res Zoom is accessible when all of the following requirements are met:
- In the video recording menu, select [FX] for [Image area] > [Choose image area],

- [ProRes 422 HQ 10-bit (MOV)], [H.265 10-bit (MOV)], [H.265 8-bit (MOV)], or [H.264 8-bit (MP4)] for [Video file type], and A frame size and rate ranging from [3840×2160; 30p] to [3840×2160; 24p] or [1920×1080; 120p] to [1920×1080; 24p].

⊹ Using Hi-Res Zoom

In the video recording menu, choose [ON] for [Hi-Res Zoom] and then zoom in or out using the left or right arrow buttons.

- When Hi-Res Zoom is activated, an icon shows on the display. When you zoom in or out, a bar appears to indicate your zoom location. You may zoom in up to 2.0×.

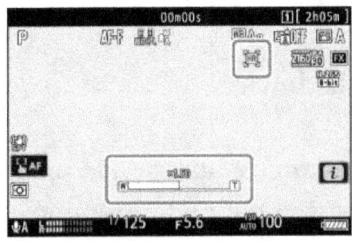

⊹ Hi-Res Zoom Cautions

The AF-area mode is locked to [Wide-area AF (L)]. The focal point is not visible.

[Electronic VR] in the movie recording option is set to [OFF].

Chapter 7: Viewing Pictures
⊹ Viewing Pictures
➢ Playback For Full-Frame

- Click the play keypad to see the most recent full-frame image in the display.

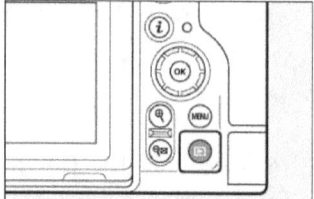

- Click the left arrow button to navigate back to the previous frame, and the right arrow button to go on to the next frame.
- To display more information about the current photo, press the up or down arrow buttons, or the DISP button.

➢ **Thumbnail Playback**

- When a full-frame image is presented, click the thumbnail playback button to examine numerous images.

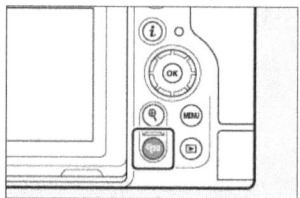

- When you click the thumbnail playback button, the number of photographs displayed grows from 4 to 9 to 72, then it lowers with each click of the zoom button.

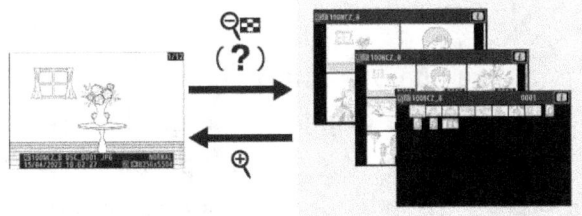

To highlight images, use the up, down, left, or right arrow buttons.

> **Touch Controls**

Touch commands can be utilized while images are presented on the monitor.

> **Auto Picture Rotation**

To show "tall" (portrait-orientation) images in tall orientation, choose [ON] for [Auto-rotate pictures] in the playback menu.

> **Reviewing Picture**

When [On] is set for [Picture review] in the replay menu, images are displayed instantly after shooting; you do not need to push the K button.

- If [On (monitor only)] is chosen, no photographs will be shown in the viewfinder.
- In continuous release settings, the display starts when the shooting stops, with the first photo in the present series displayed.
- Even when [ON] is set for [Auto-rotate photographs] in the playback menu, pictures do not rotate automatically during picture viewing.

41

> **Playback Zoom**

For zooming in on a photo in full-frame playback, use the zoom or OK buttons, or tap the display twice quickly. [FX (36×24)]-format photographs can be zoomed in up to 32× ([Large]), 24× ([Medium]), or 16× ([Small]). Faces spotted in zoom are shown by white boundaries; twist the sub-command dial to see more faces.

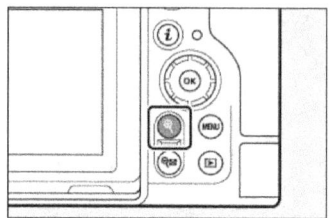

+ Making use of playback zoom

> Zoom in and Out

- To zoom in, use the zoom button or make use of the stretch gesture. To zoom out, click or use pinch movements.
- When the zoom ratio changes, a navigation window displays below the right corner of the display, with a yellow border indicating the region now viewable. The zoom ratio is displayed in a bar below the navigation window, becoming green when it reaches 1:1 (100%). The navigation window disappears off the screen after a few seconds.

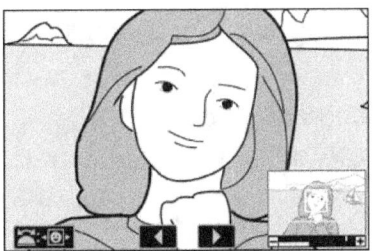

✛ View Other Areas of Picture

Use the multi-selector or glide motions to examine sections of the image that are not displayed on the monitor. Keep the multi selection held to quickly scroll to various regions of the frame.

➢ Cropping Picture

To crop the image to fit the area now displayed on the monitor, click i and choose [Quick crop].

- Face Selection

Faces spotted during zoom are marked with white outlines in the navigation pane. To display other faces, turn the sub-command dial or press the on-screen instructions.

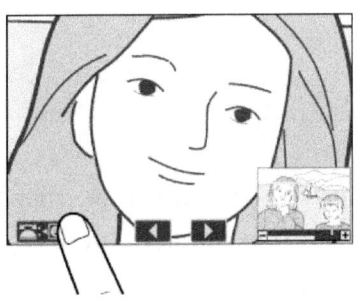

- Open Other Photos

Rotate the main command dial to see the same position in different photographs without altering your zoom ratio (selecting a video-disables zoom). You may also browse further photographs by touching the e or f icons at the bottom of the screen.

- Change to Shooting Mode

To Change, push halfway on the shutter release button or the play button.

➢ **Protecting Images from Deletion**

Pictures can be safeguarded to avoid inadvertent deletion. Protected photos will be erased when the storage device is formatted.

- Choose a Picture
    - Display the image in full-frame or playback zoom mode.
    - Alternatively, you may highlight the image in the thumbnail selection via the multi selection.
- Fn3 Button

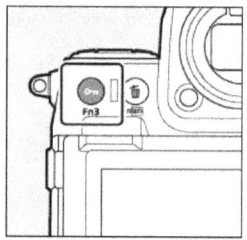

    - The P symbol indicates that a photograph is protected.
    - To remove the protection, display the image or select it in the thumbnail list, then press (Fn3) again.

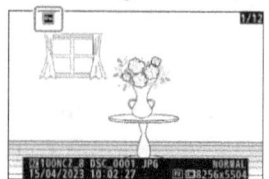

- Voice Memos
  - Protecting photographs also saves any voice notes that were recorded with the photos.
  - Voice memos cannot be safeguarded individually.

⊥ **Choosing Picture for Upload**

To upload the current photo to a mobile device, PC, or FTP server, follow the instructions outlined below.

➢ The *i* menu choices used to pick photographs for upload differ depending on the kind of device connected.

- [Choose for uploading to smart device]: This option appears when the camera is linked to a smart device via the network menu.
- [Choose for uploading to laptop]: Showed when the digital camera is linked to a computer via the network menu.
- [Choose for uploading (FTP)]: showed when the digital camera is linked to an FTP server via the network menu.
- When using the SnapBridge app to link the camera to a smart device, videos are unable to be selected for upload.
- The largest possible file size for recordings submitted using other methods is 4 GB.

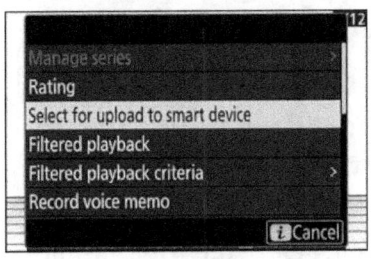

⬦ Slide Shows Viewing

Select [Slide show] from the *i* menu to see a presentation of slides in which images play again one at a time in the sequence they were recorded. You may also control how long any of the photographs in the presentation are displayed.

> **Click the *i* button after selecting the opening photo with the multi selection.**

- The slide presentation begins with the selected image and progresses through all subsequent photos.

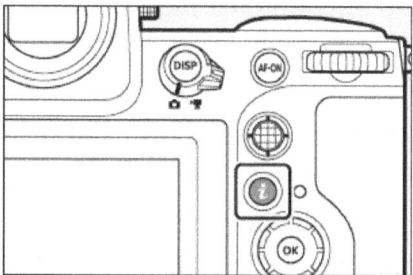

> **Select [Slide show] and hit the right arrow button.**

- To change how long photographs are shown, choose [Frame interval] and push the right arrow button.

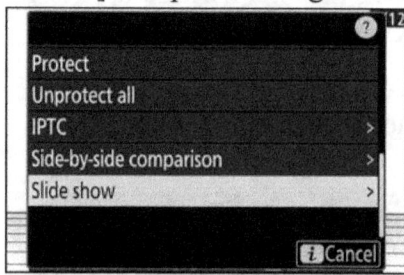

> **Select [Start] and click OK.**

- The slideshow will begin.
- For the case of movies, the [Frame interval] option is disregarded; instead, the first frame will be presented briefly before video playing begins.

- When the show concludes, a notification will appear before regular playing restarts.

✦ <u>Pictures Deleting</u>

To erase images from memory cards, follow the methods outlined below. Keep in mind that once destroyed, pictures cannot be restored; however, images that have been secured cannot be deleted either.

➤ **Making Use of the Delete Button**
- Use the multi selector to choose the desired image and then hit the delete button.
- An approval message will be presented.
- To quit without removing the image, hit OK.
- Click the delete button again the picture will be deleted

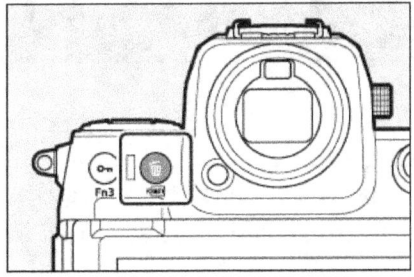

➤ **Images Captured on Selected Date**
- Use the multi selector to highlight dates and then use the left arrow button to choose them; checked box icons indicate which dates were selected. Selected dates can be deselected by clicking the left arrow button again.
- Repeat until you've chosen all of the desired dates.

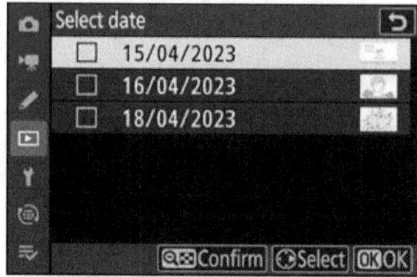

- Once you press "ok," a confirmation dialog will show up.
- To remove all of the photos that were shot on the chosen dates, highlight [Yes] and click "OK."

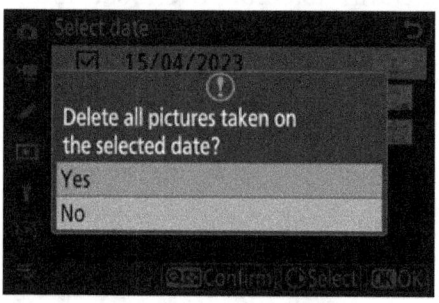

✦ Image Retouching

Existing images can be used to make retouched copies. Retouched images are saved in new files separate from the originals.

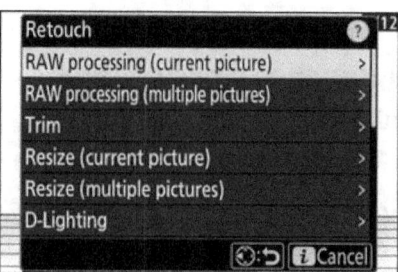

1. Choose your preferred image using the multiple selector and push the *i* button.
   - If you use [RAW processing (many photographs)] or [Resize (multiple pictures)], you won't have to

choose a picture because you will be prompted to do so later.

2. Select [Retouch] and push the right arrow key.
3. Choose the preferred option and click the right arrow key.
4. Choose retouch option
- For more information, please refer to the category for the item you have chosen.
- To quit without making a revised copy, hit K. This will take you back to the playback display.
5. Make a retouched copy.
- For more information, please refer to the category for the item you have chosen.
- Retouched copies are denoted by a mark icon.

⌕ Cautions For Retouching

The camera may be unable to show or retouch photographs that were captured or modified with another camera or on a computer.

If no action is taken for a short period of time, the display will switch off, and all unsaved modifications will be lost. To extend the time the display remains up, use Custom Setting c3 [Power off delay] > [Menus].

> ## Cautions For retouching copies
- Major items can be added to copies made with other retouching methods, although multiple modifications may result in lower image quality or odd hues.
- The impact created may vary depending on the sequence in which modifications are performed.
- Depending on the items used to generate the copy, some items may be unavailable.

- [Retouch] items in the *i* menu are grayed out and unavailable for the current photo.

Chapter 8: Video Editing

✚ <u>Video Trimming</u>

- **Remove any unneeded footage.**

1. Show a video in full frame.
2. Pause the video at the new beginning frame.
- To begin playback, press the OK button. To pause, press the down arrow key button.
- The movie progress meter indicates your approximate place in the video.
- To locate the appropriate frame, press the left or right arrow buttons or rotate the command dials.
3. Hit the *i* button, select [Trim video], and then hit the left arrow button.

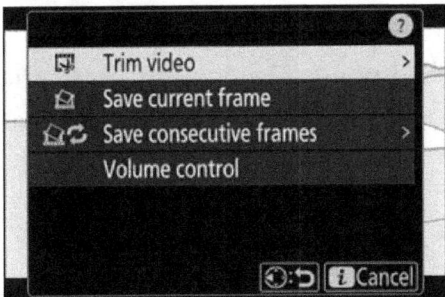

4. Select the starting place.
- To make a duplicate that starts from the present frame, select [Start point] and hit OK.

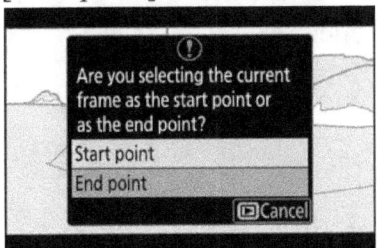

51

5. Verify the new starting point.

- If the required frame is not currently visible, use the right or left arrow buttons to advance or rewind one frame at a time.

- To skip 10 frames forward or backward, turn the principal control dial one stop.

- To skip forward or back 10 seconds, turn the sub-command dial one stop.

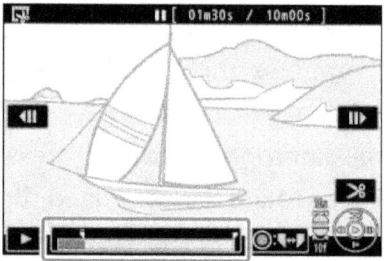

6. Select the End Point

- To access the end-point selection tool, press the center of the sub-selector, then pick the closing frame as stated in Step 5.

7. To produce a copy, click the up arrow button.
8. Pre-view the copy

- To preview the copy, select [Preview] and click OK (to stop the previewing process and return to the save choices screen, use the up arrow button).

- To exit the current duplicate and go back to Step 5, select [Cancel] and click OK.

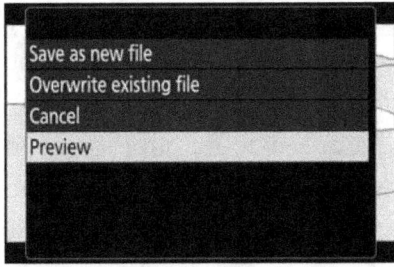

9. Select a save option.
- Select [Save as new file] for saving the altered version as a new file. For replacement of the initial video with the altered version, select [Overwrite existing file].

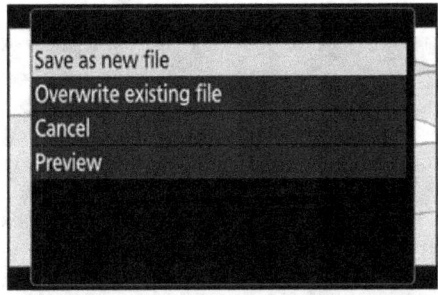

10. Save a Copy
- Click ok to save a copy of the new file

⊹ Trimming Video Precautions

- If the memory card has insufficient space, the duplicate cannot be saved.
- Videos under two seconds in length cannot be altered with [Trim video].
- Copies are created at the exact same date and time as the original.

53

♣ Save the currently active Frame as a JPEG Still.

Individual frames from existing videos can be used to produce still images. You can make one still from the present frame or a collection of stills from a specific duration of footage.

1. Pause the video at the appropriate frame.
- To pause playback, click the down arrow button.
- The movie progress meter indicates your approximate place in the video.
- To select the desired frame, press the Left or Right arrow buttons or turn the command dials.
2. Click the *i* button and select [Save current frame].
- Press OK to make a JPEG duplicate of the current frame.

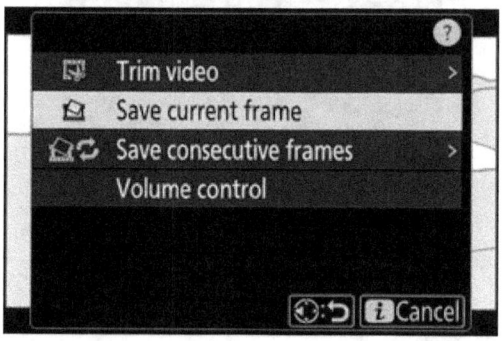

Chapter 9: HDMI TVs and Recorder connection

The digital camera can be linked to TVs, recorders, and other HDMI-equipped devices. Use an external Type A HDMI cable. The cable must be bought individually. Always turn off the camera before affixing or detaching any cables.

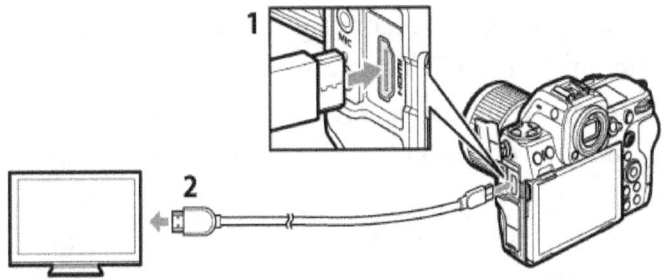

1. **HDMI connector for connecting to the camera**
2. **HDMI connector for connecting an external device.**

Select a cable with the same connector as the HDMI device.

↓ <u>TVs Connection</u>

- After setting the TV to the HDMI connection channel, turn on the camera and push the play button to see images on the screen.
- The audio playing volume can be modified using the TV's settings. The digital camera settings cannot be used.
- If the camera is linked to a smart device using the SnapBridge software, it may be utilized for controlling playback remotely when the camera is connected to a

television. For more information, see SnapBridge's online help.

- To connect to 8K-compatible televisions, use an HDMI input connector that is HDMI 2.1 compliant.

✦ Recorder

- In video mode, the recording device can record straight to the linked HDMI recorders.
- If a memory card is inserted into the camera while it is linked to a recording device, video will be recorded on both the recorder and the storage device. If no memory card is attached, the film will be recorded solely on the external device.

✦ The SnapBridge App Connection

Connect your camera to your cell phone or tablet ("smart device") via the SnapBridge app.

- For the most recent SnapBridge news, visit the Nikon website.
- Check any license terms or similar documents presented when SnapBridge begins and only proceed if you agree to them.

✦ Wireless Connection

Use the SnapBridge app to establish wireless connections across the digital camera and your smart phone or tablet. You may connect using either Bluetooth or Wi-Fi. Connecting via Bluetooth allows photos to be immediately uploaded as they are taken.

- **Bluetooth Connection (Pairing)**

Before joining over Bluetooth for the very first time, you must link the digital camera and your smartphone or tablet.

- **Before Pairing**
- Turn on Bluetooth on your smart device. For more information, refer to the device's documentation.
- Make sure that the batteries in both your camera and smart device are completely charged to avoid the gadgets turning off abruptly.
- Ensure that there is enough space on the camera's memory card.

✦ Pairing
- Connect your camera and your smartphone or tablet as instructed below.
- Some procedures are carried out using the camera, while others are on the smartphone or tablet.
- SnapBridge's online help page provides more instructions.

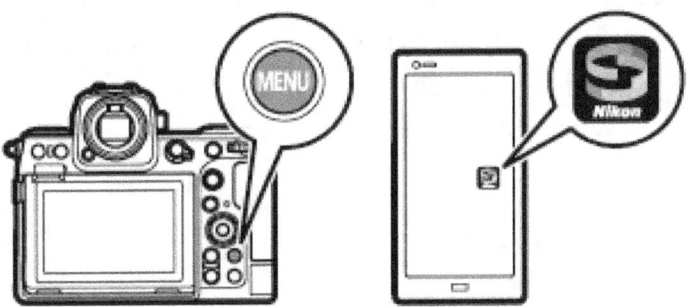

1. Camera

- In the network menu, choose [Connect to smart device] > [Pairing (Bluetooth)], then [Start pairing] and click ok.

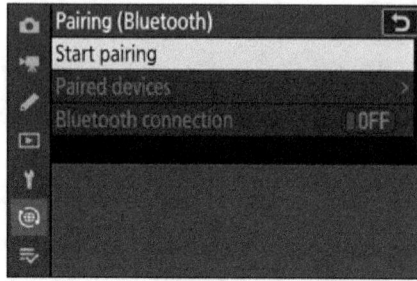

- The name of the camera will be shown on the screen of the camera.

2. Smart device

- Run the SnapBridge app and select [Connect to Camera] from the menu.
- If this is your first time using the application, you should instead tap [Connect to camera] at the welcome screen.
- When prompted, press the appropriate category for your camera, followed by the "pairing" option to select the connection type.
- When asked, tap on the camera name.

3. Smart Device/Camera

To finalize the pairing, validate that the camera and smart device show the same authentication code and then follow the prompts displayed on both devices.

- Click the pairing icon on the smart device, then push the OK button on the camera.
- When the pairing process is complete, both the camera and the smart device will show messages. The digital camera is going to automatically go to the options.

↓ Wi-Fi Mode

In Wi-Fi mode, the digital camera connects to the smartphone or tablet wirelessly, eliminating the need for Bluetooth pairing.

- Before Connecting to Wi-Fi Mode
- Enable Wi-Fi on your smartphone or tablet. For more information, refer to the device's documentation.
- Make sure the batteries in your camera and smart devices are completely charged to avoid the gadgets turning off abruptly.
- Make sure there is enough space on the camera's memory card.

↓ Connecting to a smart Device

To connect the camera to a smart device via Wi-Fi, follow the instructions outlined below.

- Some procedures are carried out using the camera, while others on the smartphone or tablet.
- SnapBridge's online help page provides more instructions.

1. Smart Device: Run the snapbridge's app on your device
- If this is your first time using the application, you should instead click [Connect to camera] at the welcome screen. Select the appropriate category for your camera, then select "Wi-Fi" as the connection type.

2. Smart Device/Camera: Put on the Camera when Prompted
    - Do not utilize any of the app's controls at this time.

3. Camera: In the network menu, choose [Connect to smart device] > [Wi-Fi connection], then highlight [Set up Wi-Fi connection] and click.

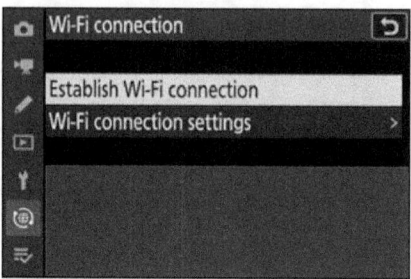

- The camera's SSID and password are going to be presented.

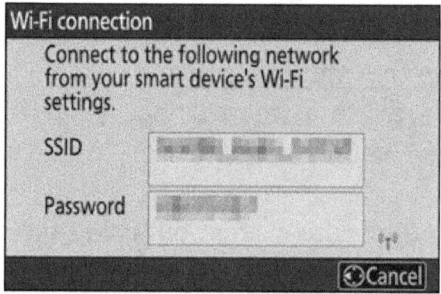

4. Smart Device: To connect to Wi-Fi, simply follow the on-screen directions.

   - On iOS devices, the "Settings" app will open. Tap [< Settings] to enter [options], then scroll up and tap [Wi-Fi] (at the very beginning of the settings list) to view Wi-Fi options.

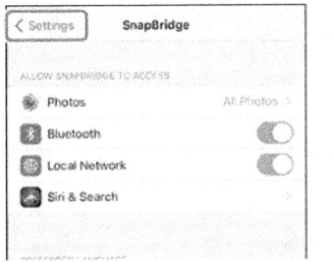 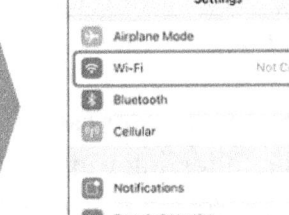

- In the Wi-Fi settings screen, pick the camera SSID and input the password provided by the camera in Step 3.

5. Smart Device: Go back to the SnapBridge app after making the necessary device settings changes (Step 4).

- After connecting to the camera via Wi-Fi, the smartphone or tablet will provide Wi-Fi mode options.
- The camera will show a message indicating that the connection between the devices is complete.

Chapter 10: Computer Connection or FTP Servers Connection

You can connect your camera to a computer or FTP Server using any of the following ways
- Computer Connection using USB
- Computer Connection via Wireless LAN
- Computer Connecting with Ethernet
- FTP Servers Connection Using Wireless LAN
- FTP Servers Connection through Ethernet

Computer Connection using USB

Pair to the camera to the computer using the included USB cord. You may then use NX Studio software to transfer photos to your PC for viewing and editing.

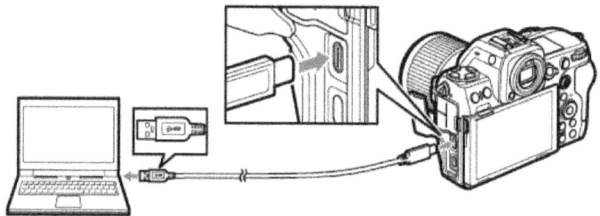

NX Studio Installation

When installing NX Studio, you will need to have an Internet connection. Visit Nikon's website for the most up-to-date information, including system specifications.
- Download the most recent NX Studio installer from their site listed below and follow the on-screen directions to finish the installation.
- https://downloadcenter.nikonimglib.com/

- It's worth noting that previous versions of NX Studio may not allow you to download photographs from the camera.

⁘ <u>Duplicating Picture to a Computer by using NX Studio</u>

1. Connecting the digital camera to a computer
   - After shutting off the camera and inserting a memory card, connect the provided USB cable as described. Make sure the cable connects to the camera's USB data connection. The computer will not recognize cameras attached via the Universal Serial Bus Power Delivery port.

2. Turning on the Camera
   - The Nikon Transfer 2 part of the NX Studio will begin. NX Studio includes the picture transmission program Nikon transmission 2.
   - If a popup appears asking users to choose a software, choose Nikon Transfer 2.
   - If Nikon Transfer 2 fails to start automatically, open NX Studio and select the "Import" button.
3. Press Start Transfer
   - Pictures from the storage device will be transferred to the computer.
4. Switched of the camera
   - Disconnect the USB cord after the transmission is complete.

⚜ Computer Connection via Wireless LAN

The camera connects to PCs using Wi-Fi (built-in wireless LAN).

➢ Multiple Device Connection

- The camera can only communicate with a single kind of device (FTP server, smart device or computer) at one time. Before trying to connect to another type of device, disconnect the present one.

➢ Cannot Connect

- If you are having difficulties connecting, try this:
- To troubleshoot, try restarting the camera or adjusting the computer's wifi settings.
- Restarting the computer.

➢ Wireless Transmitter Utility

To connect to a wireless LAN, first pair the digital camera with your computer using Nikon's Wireless Transmitter Utility program.

- Once the devices are linked, users will be able to link them to the computer via the camera.
- The Wireless Transmitter Utility can be downloaded from the Nikon Download Center. Verify your version and system requirements, and be sure you get the most recent version.
- https://downloadcenter.nikonimglib.com/

➢ Connecting the Computer through Wireless LAN

The camera may connect to computers directly (access-point mode) or through a wireless network on a current network, especially networks at home (infrastructure mode).

> **Wireless connecting directly to the camera (Access Point Mode)**

The camera and computer communicate via a direct wireless link. The camera functions as a wireless LAN access point, allowing you to connect when working outside or in other scenarios when your system is not currently connected to a wireless network, and removing the need for complex configuration changes. The PC cannot access the Internet when linked to the camera.

> **Before moving forward, verify the Wireless Transmitter Utility.**

1. Select [Link to computer] from the wireless network options, then select [Network settings] and hit the left arrow key.
2. Select [Set up a profile] and click OK.
3. Give the new profile a name
   - To go to the next stage without altering the default name, use the + button.
   - Whatever name you select will display in the [Link to computer] > [Network settings] list.
   - To change the name of the profile, hit OK. For further information on text entering, see "Text Entry". To proceed after inputting a name, use the + button.
4. Select [Direct connection to PC] and hit OK.

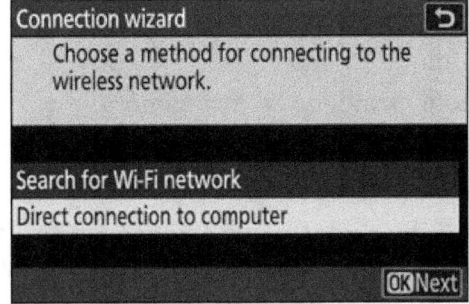

- The camera's SSID and key for encryption will be presented.

5. Create a connection with the camera.
   Windows:
   - Select the wireless LAN icon on the taskbar.
   - Choose the SSID shown by the camera's display in Step 4.
   - When requested for a network encryption key, enter the password for encryption shown by the camera in Step 4.
   - The computer will begin a connection with the camera.
   Macos:

   ➢ **Select the wireless LAN icon on the taskbar.**
   - Choose the SSID shown by the camera's display in Step 4.
   - When requested for a network encryption key, enter the password for encryption shown by the camera in Step 4. The computer will begin a connection with the camera.

6. Start Pairing
   - When asked, run the Wireless Transmitter Utility on your PC.

7. Choose the camera from the Wireless Transmitter Utility.
   - Choose the title shown by the camera's screen in Step 6 and then click [Next].

8. In your Wireless Transmitter Utility, input the authentication code provided by the camera.
   - The digital camera will show an authentication code.
   - Type in the authentication code into the Wireless Transmitter Utility dialog box and click [Next].

9. Finish the pairing procedure.
- Press OK when the camera shows a message confirming the pairing process is completed.
- In the Wireless Transmitter Utility, click [Next]. You will be requested to select a target folder. For further information, go to the Wireless Transmitter Utility's online assistance.
- When pairing is completed, the digital camera and computer will create a wireless connection.

10. Confirm the Connection
- When pairing is completed, the digital camera and computer will create a wireless connection.
- If the name for the profile does not appear in green, connect to the camera from your computer's wireless network list.

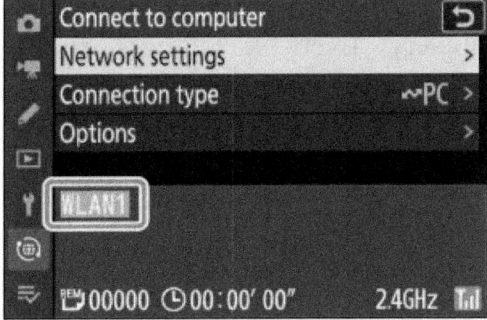

✦ Infrastructure Mode Connection

The camera communicates with a computer system on a current network (including residential networks) via a wireless router. The PC may still access the Internet while linked to the webcam.

Connections to devices outside the LAN (local area network) are not supported. You can only connect to other devices on the exact same network.

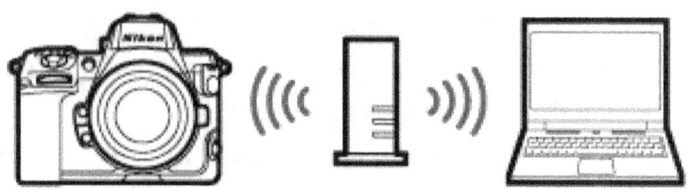

Before you continue, ensure that the Wireless Transmitter Utility is installed on your computer.

1. Select [Link to computer] from the wireless network options, then select [Network settings] and hit the left arrow key.
2. Select [Set up a profile] and click OK.
3. Give the new profile a name
   - To go to the next stage without altering the default name, use the + button.
   - Whatever name you select will display in the [Link to computer] > [Network settings] list.
   - To change the name of the profile, hit OK. For further information on text entering, see "Text Entry". To proceed after inputting a name, use the + button.
4. Select [Direct connection to PC] and hit OK.
5. Create a connection with the camera.
   Windows:
   - Select the wireless LAN icon on the taskbar.
   - Choose the SSID shown by the camera's display in Step 4.
   - When requested for a network encryption key, enter the password for encryption shown by the camera in Step 4. The computer will begin a connection with the camera.

MacOS:

- Select the wireless LAN icon on the taskbar.
- Choose the SSID shown by the camera's display in Step 4.
- When requested for a network encryption key, enter the password for encryption shown by the camera in Step 4. The computer will begin a connection with the camera.

6. Start Pairing
   - When asked, run the Wireless Transmitter Utility on your PC.

7. Choose the camera from the Wireless Transmitter Utility.
   - Choose the title shown by the camera's screen in Step 6 and then click [Next].

8. In your Wireless Transmitter Utility, input the authentication code provided by the camera.
   - The digital camera will show an authentication code.
   - Type in the authentication code into the Wireless Transmitter Utility dialog box and click [Next].

9. Finish the pairing procedure.
   - Press OK when the camera shows a message confirming the pairing process is completed.
   - In the Wireless Transmitter Utility, click [Next]. You will be requested to select a target folder. For further information, go to the Wireless Transmitter Utility's online assistance.
   - When pairing is completed, the digital camera and computer will create a wireless connection.

10. Confirm the Connection
    - When pairing is completed, the digital camera and computer will create a wireless connection.

- If the name for the profile does not appear in green, connect to the camera from your computer's wireless network list.

↓ **Computer Connecting with Ethernet**

Before you continue, ensure that the Wireless Transmitter Utility is installed on your computer. Ethernet connections require a USB (Type C) to Ethernet adapter, which is available separately from third-party vendors. Make sure you connect the adapter to the camera's USB data connection.

- The USB-to-Ethernet adapters listed below have been tested and certified for usage.
- Anker A83130A1 PowerExpand USB-C to Gigabit Ethernet Adapters
- Anker A83130A2 PowerExpand USB-C to Gigabit Ethernet Adapters
- Note that USB-to-Ethernet adapters will not function when connected to the camera's USB Power Delivery connector.

1. Connect a third-party USB-to-Ethernet adapter to the camera's USB data port and then to the PC via Ethernet cable.

- Connect your Ethernet cable to the USB-to-Ethernet adapter. Avoid using force or attempting to insert the connections at an angle.
- Connect the opposite end of the wire to your computer or router.

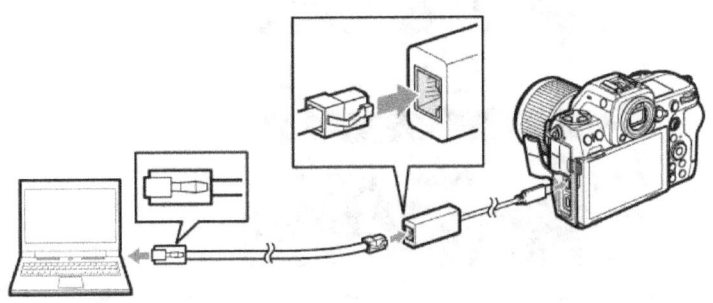

2. In the network option, select [USB-LAN] instead of [USB data connection].
3. In the network menu, choose [Connect to computer], then choose [Network settings] and hit OK.
4. Select [Create profile] and push OK.
5. Choose a name for the new profile.
   - To go to the next stage without altering the default name, use the + button.
   - Whatever name you select will display in the [Connect to computer] > [The network settings] list.
   - To change the name of the profile, hit OK. Refer to "Text Entry" for further details. To proceed after inputting a name, use the + button.
   - There might be a delay before the device identifies the USB-to-Ethernet adaptor. If the camera does not identify an Ethernet connection, the wizard will create a wireless local area network profile with the default name "WLAN1".
6. Select or obtain an IP address
   - Select one of the choices below and hit OK.
     i. Enter Manually
     ii. Obtain Automatically

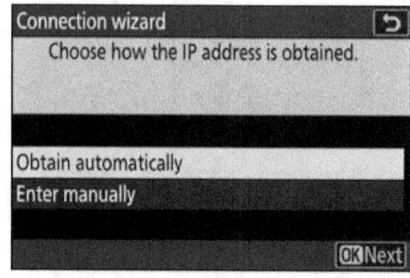

7. When you get the "configuration complete" notification, press OK to proceed.
8. Start Pairing
    • When asked, run the Wireless Transmitter Utility on your PC.
9. Choose the camera from the Wireless Transmitter Utility.
    • Choose the name shown by the camera's display in Step 8 and press [Next].
10. Enter the camera-displayed authentication code into the Wireless Transmitter Utility.
    • The webcam will show a verification code.
    • Input the verification code into the Wireless Transmitter Utility dialog box and click [Next].
11. Finish the pairing procedure.
    • When the camera shows a message indicating that the pairing has been finished, tap OK.
    • In the Wireless Transmitter Utility, click [Next]. You will be requested to select a target folder. For further information, go to the Wireless Transmitter Utility's online assistance.
    • When the pairing is complete, the computer and the digital camera will create a connection.
12. Verify the connection.
    • Once a connection is made, the profile name will appear in green on the camera's option.

✦ Finishing the connection to the computer

You may terminate the connection by:

- To turn off the camera or,
- Select [Stop current connection] in the [Connect to computer] > [Network settings] menu.

- **FTP Servers Connection Using Wireless LAN**
- **FTP Servers Connection through Ethernet**

✦ FTP Servers Connection Using Wireless LAN

The camera may connect to FTP servers via a direct wireless connection link (access-point mode) or through a wireless router that is installed on an existing network, even home networks (architecture mode).

- **FTP Servers**

- Servers may be setup using conventional FTP services such as IIS (Internet Information Services), which are included with Windows 11 and Windows 10.
- Internet FTP connections and FTP server connections via third-party applications are not supported.
- Before connecting to a server using FTPS, you must put a root certification onto the camera. This may be accomplished by selecting [Connect to FTP server] > [Options] > [Manage root certificate] > [Import root certificate] from the network menu.
- For more information on obtaining root certificates, contact a network administrator of the relevant FTPS server.

↓ Straight connection via wireless (Access-Point Mode)

The camera and FTP server communicate via a direct wireless connection. The camera functions as a wireless LAN access point, allowing you to connect when working outside or in other scenarios when the FTP server is not already linked to a wireless network, and removing the need for complex configuration changes.

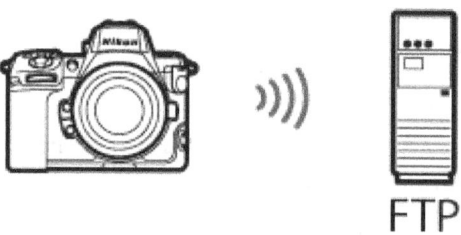

- Make a host profile with the camera connection wizard.

1. From the network menu, select [Connect to FTP server], then select [Network settings] and hit the right arrow key.

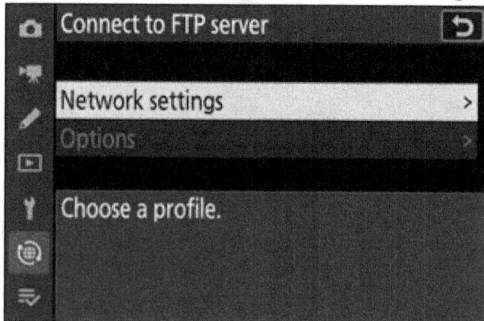

2. Select [Set up a profile] and then press OK.

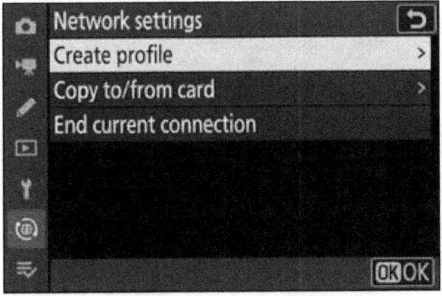

3. Select [Connection wizard] and use the right arrow button.

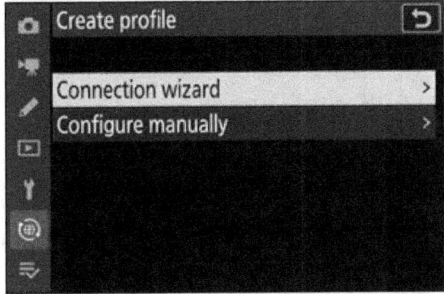

- The connecting wizard will start.

4. Give the profile a name

- To go to the next stage without altering the default name, use the + button.
- Whatever name you select will display in the [Connect to FTP server] > [Network settings] list.
- To change the name of the profile, hit OK. For further information on text entering, see "Text Entry". To proceed after inputting a name, use the + button.

5. Select [Send link to computer] and then push ok.

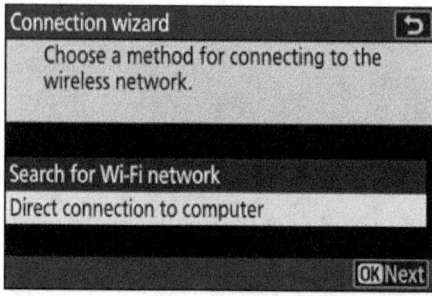

- The SSID of the camera and its encryption key will be shown.

6. Create a connection with the camera.

   Windows:
   - Select the wireless LAN icon on the taskbar.
   - Choose the SSID shown by the camera's display in Step 5.
   - When requested for a network encryption key, enter the password for encryption shown by the camera in Step 4.
   - The computer will begin a connection with the camera.

   MacOS:

   - Select the wireless LAN icon on the taskbar.
   - Choose the SSID shown by the camera's display in Step 5.
   - When requested for a network encryption key, enter the password for encryption shown by the camera in Step 5. The computer will begin a connection with the camera.

7. Select the server type
   ➤ Select [FTP], [SFTP] (SSH FTP), or [FTPS] (FTP-SSL) and click OK to bring up a window where you can select a login method.

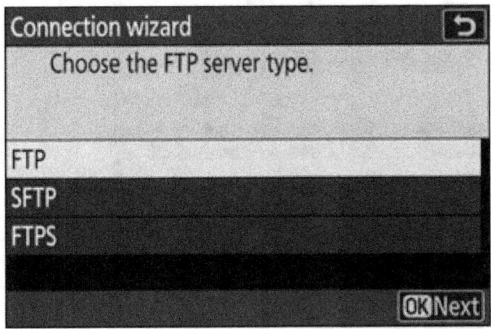

8. Login
   • Select one of the choices below and hit ok.

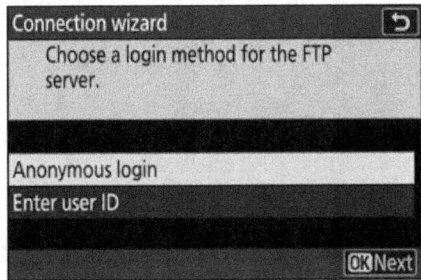

➢ Anonymous Login
   • Choose this selection if the server's configuration doesn't ask for a username or password. This option is only available on servers set for anonymous login. If your login succeeds, the camera will ask you to select a destination.
➢ Enter User ID
   • Enter your username and password. When you've finished entering information, click OK to log in. If your login succeeds, the camera will ask you to select a destination.
9. Select a destination folder.
   • Select any of the following options and hit OK.

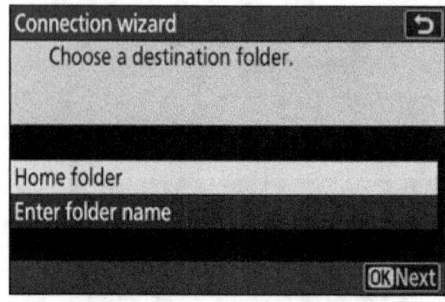

➢ Home Folder
  • Select this option to make the server's home folder the destination for images transferred from the camera. If the procedure is successful, you will get a "setup complete" popup.
➢ Enter Folder Name
  • Enter the target folder's name manually. The directory must already be on the server. When requested, provide the folder name and path, then click ok to bring up the "setup complete" window.

10. Check the connection
When the connection is made, the profile name is highlighted in green in the camera's [Connect to FTP server] option.

Chapter 11: Custom Settings Menu

To see Custom Settings, go to the camera menus and pick the pen tab.

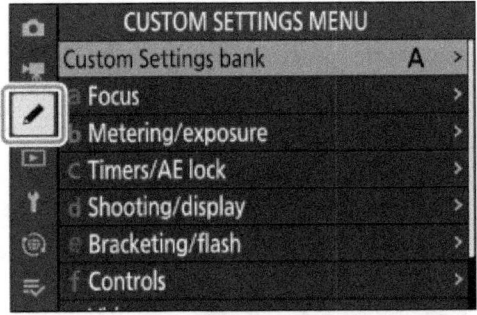

Custom Settings are utilized to tailor camera settings to particular needs. There are two layers to the Custom Settings menu.

✛ The Custom Settings Bank

Custom Settings are saved in one of the four banks (banks "A" through "D"), which may be accessed via [Custom Settings bank]. Changes to settings made when one bank is selected do not affect the remaining banks.

➢ **Changing the names of Custom Settings banks**
- To add a descriptive description to the bank name ("A", "B", "C", or "D"), highlight it, hit the right arrow key, and choose [Rename]. The captions can be up to twenty characters long.

➢ **Copying the Custom Settings Banks.**
- To make a duplicate of a custom settings bank, select it, press the right arrow key, click [duplicate], and provide a location for the copy.

➢ **Restoring the default settings.**
- You can restore the initial settings for a certain Custom Settings bank. To accomplish this, highlight the bank and

hit the delete button; a confirmation box will appear. To restore the initial settings for the selected bank, highlight [Yes] and hit OK.

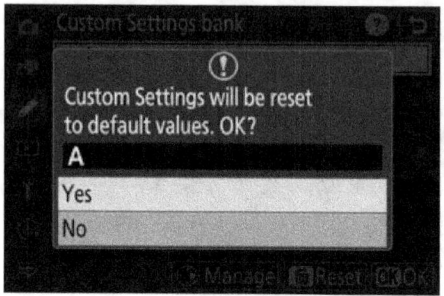

⊥ a1: AF-C Priority Selection

When using AF-C, decide whether images can be shot before the camera focuses.

> **Release**
>   • Photos may be shot anytime the shutter button is touched (release priority).
> **Focus Release**
>   • Priority is usually given to release, however if the subject is dark or has poor contrast & the digital camera is in continuous-release mode of operation, priority is given to focus for the first image in each series. For any additional shots, release will be prioritized above focus. This ensures that the initial photo of each series is in focus.
> **Focus**
>   • Photos can only be taken while the camera is focused (focus priority).

a2: AF-C Priority Selection

- When using AF-S, you may specify whether images can be shot before the camera focuses.

  - **Release**
    - Photos may be shot anytime the shutter button is touched (release priority).
  - **Focus**
    - Photos can only be taken while the camera is focused (focus priority).

a3: Locked-on focus tracking

- When using AF-C focus mode, you may adjust how rapidly the focus responds to changes among the object in focus and the camera.

  ➤ **Blocked Shot AF Response**

- Pick [5] ([Delayed]) to help you stay focused on your original topic.
- Select [1] ([Quick]) to enable it easier for you to shift attention to things that cross your range of vision.
- When [3D-tracking] is set for AF-area mode, blocked shot AF response operates in mode [3], regardless of the choice chosen.
- If [Auto-area AF] is set for AF-area mode, the blocked shot AF reaction will operate in mode [3] when [2] or [1] is chosen.

  ➤ **Subject Motion**

- Steady

When capturing subjects which approach the camera steadily, opt for smooth focus.

- Erratic

When capturing object that are prone to quick starts and pauses, choose better responsiveness.

✦ a4: Focus Point used

When selecting a choice other than [Auto-area AF] for AF-area mode, specify the amount of points of focus accessible via manual focus-point selection.

- All Points

You can pick any focus point accessible in the current AF-area mode. The amount of points accessible depends on the AF-area mode.

- Alternative Points

Whenever [All points] is selected, the number of potential focus points is limited to one-quarter of the original amount. Use for rapid focus point selection. The amount of available points for [Pinpoint AF] is unaffected.

✦ a5: Store Point by Orientation

Select whether distinct focus points can be used for "wide" (landscape) orientation, "tall" (portrait) orientation with the camera rotated 90° clockwise, and "tall" orientation with the camera rotated 90° counterclockwise.

- Choose [Off] to maintain the same focus point independent of camera orientation.

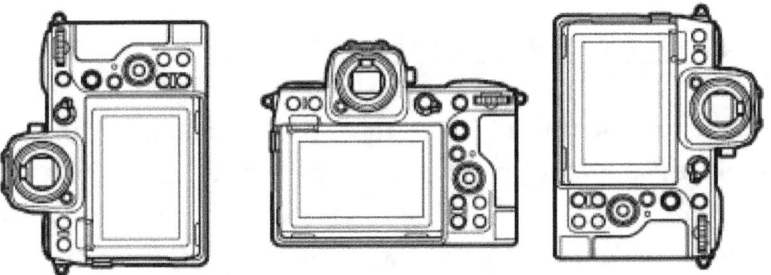

- To allow independent selection of the focus point and the AF-area mode, select [Focus point and AF-area mode].

✦ a6: AF Activation

Select if the button to release the shutter may be used to focus.

- Shutter/AF ON

When you click the shutter release button halfway, the camera will focus.

- AF ON Only

When you click the shutter release button halfway, the camera does not focus.

Selecting [AF-ON only] and using the right arrow key bring up [Out-of-focus release] choices.

- Enables

Photos may be shot anytime the shutter button is touched (release priority).

- Disable
  - o To shoot photos, the camera must be in focus (focus priority).

o Use the AF-ON button or designated controls to focus.

⊹ a7: Focus Point Persistence

The custom Setting f2 [Custom controls (shooting)] allows you to select if the focus point selected by the camera remains in use after changing AF-area modes. This only occurs if you switch AF-area modes when aiming with the shutter-release button held halfway.

- Auto

The previous focus point selected by the camera before switching AF-area modes stays in effect.
- Off

The last focus point selected by the user returns to normal.
Focus-point persistence occurs when you transition from an AF-area mode, such as [Auto-area AF], whereby the focus point is selected automatically, to one in wherein the focus point is chosen manually.

⊹ a8: Limit AF-Area Mode Selection
Select the AF-area modes by pushing the focus-mode button and moving the subcommand dial.

- To pick or deselect choices, highlight them and then hit the ok or right arrow keys. The sub-command dial allows you to pick modes marked with a checkmark.
- To finish the process, hit MENU.

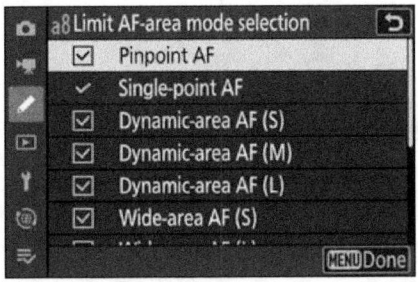

⊹ a9: Focus Mode Restriction

Select only one focus mode. If a different choice than [No limitations] is selected, turning the main control dial when pressing the focus-mode button will not alter the focus mode.

⊹ a10: Focus Point Wrap Around

Select whether focus-point selection "wraps around" from one end of the display to the next. When [ON] is chosen, focus-point selection will "wrap around" from up to down, bottom to top, right to left, and left to right, so that using the right arrow button when a focus point on the right edge of the display is highlighted picks the equivalent point on the left edge.

Chapter 12: Technical Note

⊥ Compatible Accessories and Lenses

All Z-mount lenses are compatible with the camera.
Make sure you keep your camera and lens firmware up to date.
Some capabilities may not be available in previous versions, and
the camera may fail to recognize the lens correctly.

➤ Compatible F Mount Lenses

An FTZ II/FTZ mount adaptor allows F mount lenses to be
installed on Z mount cameras.

- Certain functionalities may be unavailable according to
  the lens used.
- Compatible F Mount Lenses provides information about
  F mount lenses that may be used with Z mount cameras,
  as well as any restrictions that may apply. Nikon's
  Download Center offers compatible F Mount lenses.

➤ Other Compatible Accessories

There are several accessories provided to use with your Nikon
camera.

- Accessibility might differ by nation or region.
- For the most up-to-date information, visit our website or
  consult our brochures.

  - Power Sources
  o EN-EL15c Nikon Z 8 digital cameras support
    rechargeable Li-ion batteries (EN-EL15c).

o EN-EL15b and EN-EL15a batteries can also be utilized. However, fewer photos can be shot on a single charge compared to the EN-EL15c.

o The MH-25a Battery Charger can recharge EN-EL15c batteries.

o The EH-7P Charging AC Adapter and EH-8P AC Adapter attach to the camera's USB Power Delivery connection and charge batteries.

 o The battery will not charge when the camera is turned on.

 o The EH-7P and EH-8P cannot charge EN-EL15A batteries.

 o To power the camera, use the EH-7P or EH-8P. In the settings menu, select [ON] for [USB power delivery]. For further information, see "USB Power Delivery".

 o To power the camera with an EH-8P, a UC-E25 USB cable is required (sold separately).

o To power the device for longer durations, use the EH-5d AC adapter with the EP-5B power connector.

o The MB-N12 Power Battery Pack is a battery pack for the Nikon Z8 digital camera. When installed, it supports up to two EN-EL15c rechargeable Li-ion batteries for power.

 o The MB-N12 includes keys, buttons, and a multi selector for use when the digital camera is turned to shoot portrait ("tall") photos.

- Filters

- To preserve the lens, use Neutral Color (NC) filters.

- Whenever a picture is framed with a bright light or there is a strong light source in the frame, filters might induce ghosting. If you see ghosting, you can remove the filters.

- Filters designed for special effects Photography could cause issues with the in-focus indication or autofocus.

✦ Remote terminal Accessories

The camera has a ten-pin remote connector that allows for remote control and automated photography.

Replace the terminal cover whenever the terminal ceases to be in use. Dust or other foreign matter that accumulates in the terminal contacts can trigger the camera to malfunction.

- MC-22/MC-22A Remote Cords (about 1 meter/3.3 feet): Detached shutter releases have blue, yellow, and black terminals for connecting to remote camera-triggering devices, which can be controlled by sound or electronic signals.
- MC-30/MC-30A remote cords (about 80 cm/2.7 ft) provide remote shutter releases and help decrease camera vibration.
- MC-36/MC-36A Remote Cords (about 85 cm/2.8 ft): Remote shutter triggers with timers for interval-timed photography.

✦ USB Cables

- The UC-E24 USB Cable includes a Type C connector for connecting to your camera with a Type A connector for connecting to the USB device.
- UC-E25 USB Cable: This USB cable has two Type C connections.

⊹ Hot Shoe Adaptor
- AS-15 Sync Terminal Adapter: Place the AS-15 on the camera's hot shoe to attach studio flashing lights or other flashing devices via a sync terminal.

  - Accessories Shoe Cover
- AS-15 Sync Terminal Adapter: Place the AS-15 on the camera's hot shoe to attach studio flashing lights or other flashing devices via a sync terminal.

  - Body Cap
- The BF-N1 Body Cap prevents dust from entering the camera while no lens is installed.

⊹ View-Finder Eyepiece Accessories
- DK-33 Rubber Eyecup: The camera comes with a rubber eyecup. It may be removed by pushing the eyepiece unlock (1) and turning the eyecup in the direction indicated (2).

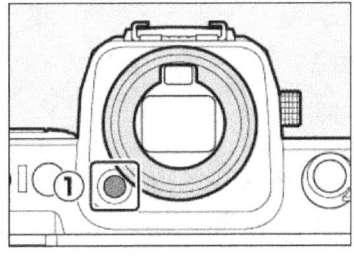 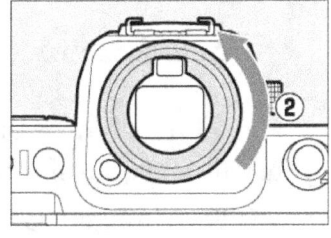

- To reattach the eyecup, line the mark on the back of the eyecup (4) against the sign on the camera's body (3) and spin it as described until it snaps into place (5).

⥥ Microphones

- Connect the ME-1 Stereo Microphone to the camera's microphone jack to capture stereo audio. via an external microphone also lowers the possibility of getting up device noise, such as the sounds made while video recording if focus is established via autofocus.
- ME-W1 Wireless Microphone: A Bluetooth-enabled microphone. Use the ME-W1 for off-camera recordings.

⥥ Remote Grip

The MC-N10 Remote Grip, when attached to the camera, may be utilized for functions such as video recording, photography, and modifying camera settings. It has a rosette for easy connection to outside camera accessories. having the MC-N10 attached on outside camera accessories via an ARRI-compatible rosette adapter, you can continue to keep moving subjects in focus while panning the camera to follow their motion, or use the conveniently placed controls to adjust settings like exposure and white balance without touching the camera.

⥥ Caring for the Camera

- Long Term Storage

If you will not be using the product for an extended length of time, remove the battery. While taking the battery out, ensure that the camera is turned off.

- Do not keep the camera in areas that:
- Poor ventilation or over 60% humidity
- Exposure to powerful electromagnetic fields (e.g., televisions or radios)
- Exposure to temperatures exceeding 50°C (122°F) or below -20°C (-4°F).

↓ Cleaning

The technique differs depending on the part that needs cleaning. The processes are outlined below.

- Avoid using alcohol, thinners, or other volatile substances.

➤ Body of the Camera

To get rid of dust and lint, use a blower, then gently clean using a soft, dry cotton. After handling your camera at a beach or seashore, remove any sand or salt using a cloth gently soaked with distilled water and completely dry the camera.

Important: Dirt or other substance within the camera might cause the device to fail. The warranty does not cover damage caused by the presence of extraneous substance within the camera.

➤ View-finder and Lenses

These glass parts can be easily damaged; use a blower to clear dust and lint. When using a blower, keep the can upright to avoid liquid discharge, which might harm glass elements. To get rid of fingerprints and other stains, add a tiny quantity of lens cleaning to a cotton towel and carefully clean.

➤ The Monitor

Use a blower to remove dust and lint. To remove smudges, finger prints, and other greasy stains, gently wipe the surface using a soft fabric or chamois leather. Avoid using pressure, since this may cause damage or malfunction.

➢ Cleaning the image Sensor

Dirt or dust that enters the camera when the lens is changed or the body cover is removed may attach to the imaging sensor and impair your images. The "clean image sensor" option shakes the sensor to eliminate dust.

The image sensor may be cleaned manually from the settings or instantly once the camera is switched off. If image sensor cleaning does not address the issue, call a Nikon-authorized service person.

➢ Making Use of The Menus

- Set the device in the typical position (base down) for the best results.

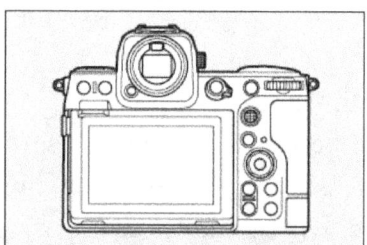

- Choose [Clean image sensor] from the settings menu, then select [Start] and click to start cleaning.
- The camera adjustments cannot be utilized while the cleaning process is underway. Do not unplug or remove the power supply.
- When the cleaning process is completed, the configuration menu will appear.

➤ Manual Cleaning

If substance that cannot be eliminated from the image sensor by image sensor cleaning, the image sensor can be manually cleaned as indicated below. However, the sensor is highly fragile and easily damaged;

1. Turn off the camera and detach the lens.
2. Positioning the camera upright so that light may enter, check the photographic sensor for dirt or lint.
3. Use a blower to eliminate any dust or fuzz from the sensor.
   - Avoid using a blower brush. The bristles might harm the sensor.
   - Only Nikon-authorized service experts can remove dirt that a blower cannot remove. You should never touch or wipe the sensor.

4. Reinstall the lens or the provided body cap.

Index